A VISIT TO THE
United Kingdom

REVISED AND UPDATED

UNITED
KINGDOM

EUROPE

NORTH
AMERICA

ASIA

AFRICA

SOUTH
AMERICA

AUSTRALIA

Rachael Bell

Heinemann
LIBRARY

www.heinemann.co.uk/library

Visit our website to find out more information about Heinemann Library books.

To order:

☎ Phone 44 (0) 1865 888066

📄 Send a fax to 44 (0) 1865 314091

💻 Visit the Heinemann Bookshop at www.heinemann.co.uk/library to browse our catalogue and order online.

First published in Great Britain by Heinemann Library, Halley Court, Jordan Hill, Oxford OX2 8EJ, part of Pearson Education. Heinemann is a registered trademark of Pearson Education Ltd.

Editorial: Diyan Leake
Design: Joanna Hinton-Malivoire and Philippa Jenkins
Picture research: Mica Brancic
Production: Duncan Gilbert

Originated by Chroma Graphics (Overseas) Pte Ltd
Printed and bound in China by South China Printing Co. Ltd

ISBN 978 0 431 087368 (hardback)
12 11 10 09 08
10 9 8 7 6 5 4 3 2 1

ISBN 978 0 431 087504 (paperback)
12 11 10 09 08
10 9 8 7 6 5 4 3 2 1

British Library Cataloguing in Publication Data

Bell, Rachael, 1972 –
A visit to the United Kingdom. – New ed.
1. Great Britain – Social conditions – 21st century – Juvenile literature 2. Great Britain – Geography – Juvenile literature 3. Great Britasin – Social life and customs – 21st century – Juvenile literare
I. Title II. The United Kingdom
941'.086

Acknowledgements

The publishers would like to thank the following for permission to reproduce photographs: © Ace Photo Agency p. **8** (Geoff Smith); © Alamy pp. **10** (Alan Copson City Pictures), **12** (Dave Pattison), **14** (Adrian Sherratt), **25** (Jeff Morgan Education); © Anthony Blake Photo Library p. **13** (Gerrit Buntrock); © Aviemore Photographic p. **27**; © Collections p. **6** (Gena Davies); © Corbis p. **11** (Arcaid/Charlotte Wood); © Images Colour Library pp. **5**, **7**; © J. Allan Cash Ltd pp. **15**, **17**, **19**, **21**, **22**, **23**, **24**, **26**, **29**; © Link p. **16** (Orde Eliason); © Shakespeare's Globe p. **28**; © Tony Stone Images p. **20** (Penny Tweedie); © Trip pp. **9** (P. Rauter), **18** (C. Kapolka).

Cover photograph reproduced with permission of © Lonely Planet Images/Anders Blomqvist.

Our thanks to Nick Lapthorn for his comments in the preparation of this book.

Every effort has been made to contact copyright holders of any material reproduced in this book. Any omissions will be rectified in subsequent printings if notice is given to the publishers.

Contents

Any words appearing in bold, **like this**, are explained in the Glossary.

The United Kingdom

The United Kingdom is made up of a large island called **Great Britain**, part of Ireland, and lots of little islands.

People call the United Kingdom "the UK", for short. There are four different areas in the UK that used to be separate countries. These are England, Northern Ireland, Scotland, and Wales.

There are small villages in the UK as well as big cities.

Land

The north of **Great Britain** has mountains and deep valleys and lakes. In the south, there are gentle hills with wide rivers, where it is easier to grow crops.

There is lots of rain on the high land in the west of the country. Rain makes the grass and plants grow well there.

There are deep and wide valleys in Wales.

Landmarks

The Giant's Causeway in Northern Ireland is a strange **volcanic** rock on the coast. **Legend** says it was a giant's road that was built to step over the sea into Scotland.

The Tower of London was once a prison castle.

London, the **capital** of the UK, has many famous buildings. Many **tourists** go to see the **keepers** and the **crown jewels** at the Tower of London.

Homes

Most people in the UK live in houses in towns or cities. Many of these houses were built over 100 years ago.

Some people live in blocks of flats. New ones are being built and some empty old buildings in city centres are being made into flats.

These flats are in the east of London.

Food

You will find a fish and chip shop in every town. Because the UK is an island, fishermen supply fresh fish throughout the year. Chips are a popular snack.

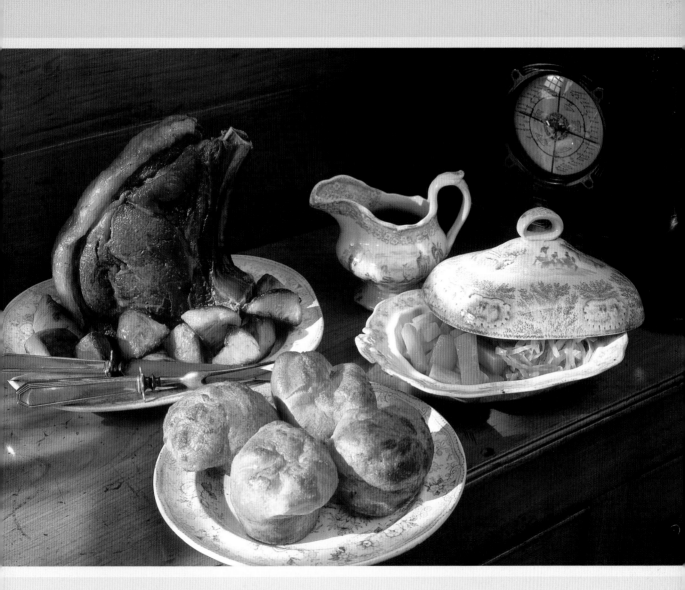

Different parts of the UK have their own special dishes but many families enjoy a **traditional** Sunday lunch. This is a big piece of cooked meat, which is eaten with potatoes, other vegetables, and **gravy**.

Clothes

Many famous **fashion designers** come from the UK. Young people enjoy wearing modern, fashionable clothes. Sports clothes are also very popular.

There are hundreds of
different tartan patterns.

One of the **traditional** clothes in the UK
is the **tartan** kilt. This is a checked, wool
skirt worn by Scottish men and women
on special occasions.

Work

Eight out of ten people in the UK work in a service industry. This means that they work in transport, **education**, health and leisure, or money-related work.

Most other people work in industry.
This means that they help to make
or build things such as cars. Very few
people work in farming in the UK.

Transport

The London Underground was opened over 100 years ago. It used **steam trains** at first. Now it uses electricity. Three million people travel on it every day.

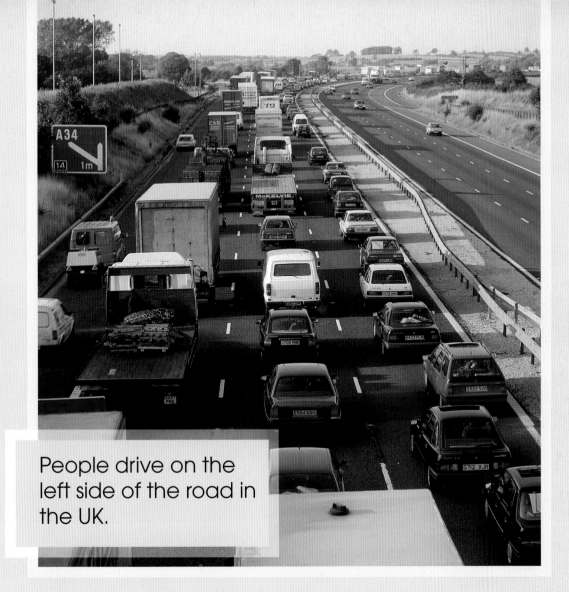

People drive on the left side of the road in the UK.

Most people travel to work by car and goods are transported by lorry. This means that the roads and motorways are very busy and there is a lot of **pollution**.

Languages

Almost everybody in the UK speaks English. Each area has a different **accent**. Sometimes it can be hard for people from different areas to understand each other.

Street signs in Wales are in both Welsh and English.

In the UK about 750 thousand people speak Welsh and some people speak **Gaelic**. Some people speak other languages because their parents or grandparents came from other countries.

School

Children have to go to school from the age of 5 until they are 16. They study science, geography, history, English, music, maths, art, and physical education.

In some schools students wear a jacket called a blazer.

Most schools are free and children from the local area go there. Some schools charge parents money and sometimes the children live there during the school terms.

Free time

Many famous sports, such as football, tennis, and cricket, have come from the UK. Children play these both in and out of school. Adults also play these sports in their free time.

Many people enjoy being outdoors. Some go to the beach in summer. Others go walking or cycling in the mountains in the Lake District or Scotland.

These people are enjoying being outdoors in Wales.

Celebrations

The biggest celebration of the whole year is Christmas. The streets are lit with Christmas lights. People buy presents for each other and eat special Christmas food.

Burns Night is on 25 January every year.

Another special celebration in Scotland is Burns Night. People wear **tartan** clothes, and eat a special food called haggis. They listen to **bagpipe** music.

The Arts

The UK is famous for its theatre. The plays of **Shakespeare** are very well known all around the world. Also, there are many theatres and theatre festivals.

Wales is famous for its **male voice choirs**.

The UK has many musicians and pop groups. In Wales the Eisteddfod festival is a big competition for people who sing, write poetry, or play music.

Factfile

Name	The full name of the UK is the United Kingdom of **Great Britain** and Northern Ireland.
Capital	The **capital** city of the UK is London.
Language	Most people speak English, but some also speak Welsh or Gaelic.
Population	There are about 60 million people living in the United Kingdom.
Money	Money in the UK is the pound (£), which is divided into 100 pence. Scotland and Wales also have their own coins and bank notes.
Religions	There are many Christians in the UK, as well as Muslims, Sikhs, Hindus, Jews, and Buddhists.
Products	The UK produces oil and gas, wheat and other foods, chemicals, cars, and other transport machinery.

Welsh words you can learn

diolch (DEE-olkh)	thank you
bore da (boh-re-DAR)	good morning
nos da (norse-dar)	good night
hwyl fawr (hooeel-vowr)	goodbye
ie (EE-eh)/na (nar)	yes/no

Glossary

accent a different way of saying the same word

bagpipes a musical instrument that you blow. It has pipes and a bag to collect the air

capital the city where the government is based

crops the plants that farmers grow and harvest (gather)

crown jewels the crowns and special jewels worn by the Queen of Great Britain

education anything to do with teaching children or adults

fashion designers people who draw ideas for clothes which are then made

Gaelic the ancient language of the people who first lived in Scotland, Ireland, Wales, and Breton in France

gravy meat juices that are made into a sauce

Great Britain an large island in Europe where England, Scotland, and Wales are

keepers people who wear special clothes and protect a building

legend a well-known, old story

male voice choir group of men who get together to sing

pollution dirt and poisons that fill the air, usually made by car and lorry engines

Shakespeare a man who lived over 400 years ago. He wrote plays and poems that are still popular today.

steam train an old type of train that burned coal to make steam which made the engine work

tartan woollen cloth with a check pattern in different colours

tourist person who is travelling to other places for holidays or to see the sights

traditional the way things have been done or made for a long time

volcanic a type of rock that has melted and is pushed out from beneath the Earth's surface

Index